THE POETRY OF GOLD

The Poetry of Gold

Walter the Educator

Silent King Books

SILENT KING BOOKS

SKB

"Earning a degree in chemistry changed my life!"
– Walter the Educator
dedicated to all the chemistry lovers, like myself, across the world

GOLD

Gold gleams, a treasure from ages past.

GOLD

Its radiant hue, a luminous sheen,

GOLD

In tales of splendor, it reigns supreme.

GOLD

From deep within Earth's silent embrace,

GOLD

Gold emerges with ethereal grace.

GOLD

Born from the crucible's fiery kiss,

GOLD

Its essence woven in nature's bliss.

GOLD

A metal rare, in scarcity prized,

GOLD

Yet in its allure, secrets disguised.

GOLD

In sun-kissed rivers and mountain streams,

GOLD

Gold whispers softly, in radiant dreams.

GOLD

Upon the alchemist's ancient scroll,

GOLD

Gold's mysteries writ, a sacred toll.

GOLD

Transmutation sought, in quest sublime,

GOLD

To turn base into gold, through space and time.

GOLD

In alchemic fires, it dances free,

GOLD

A symbol of wealth, of potency.

GOLD

But beyond mere riches, its essence lies,

GOLD

In the depths of souls, where truth defies.

GOLD

Golden sunsets paint the evening sky,

GOLD

As whispers of eternity fly.

GOLD

In each golden moment, life's tales unfold,

GOLD

In melodies of love, and stories untold.

GOLD

A treasure trove of legends untamed,

GOLD

In gold's embrace, destinies framed.

GOLD

From Pharaoh's tombs to modern delight,

GOLD

Gold's shimmering touch ignites the night.

GOLD

In the hands of kings, it crowns their might,

GOLD

Yet in humble hearts, it shines just as bright.

GOLD

For in its allure, a mirror we see,

GOLD

Reflecting the soul's true majesty.

GOLD

Golden dreams in the miner's eye,

GOLD

As veins of fortune beneath Earth lie.

GOLD

Through toil and sweat, they seek the prize,

GOLD

In the golden depths where dreams arise.

GOLD

But beware the lure of greed's embrace,

GOLD

For gold's allure can lead to disgrace.

GOLD

In hearts consumed by avarice's flame,

GOLD

The golden gleam tarnishes with shame.

GOLD

Yet in the crucible of trials endured,

GOLD

Gold's purity shines, forever secured.

GOLD

For in the fires of adversity's test,

GOLD

True gold emerges, at its best.

GOLD

ABOUT THE CREATOR

Walter the Educator is one of the pseudonyms for Walter Anderson. Formally educated in Chemistry, Business, and Education, he is an educator, an author, a diverse entrepreneur, and he is the son of a disabled war veteran. "Walter the Educator" shares his time between educating and creating. He holds interests and owns several creative projects that entertain, enlighten, enhance, and educate, hoping to inspire and motivate you.

Follow, find new works, and stay up to date
with Walter the Educator™
at WaltertheEducator.com

9 798869 264176